Paul Revere's Ride

*The Thrilling Midnight Dash That
Ignited Revolution & American
Courage*

A Modern Translation
Adapted for the Contemporary Reader

Henry Wadsworth Longfellow

Translated by Tim Zengerink

Table of Contents

Preface
Message to the Reader

Rebuilding the Greatest Library in Human History

Thousands of years ago, the Library of Alexandria was the heart of global knowledge — a sanctuary where the wisdom of every known civilization was gathered and shared freely.

And then, it was lost.

Now, we're rebuilding it — and you are invited to join us.

At the Library of Alexandria, we've set out to make every book available to every person on Earth — not just in print, but in every language, every format, and for every reader.

Here's how we do it:

- **Deluxe Print Editions at True Printing Cost** - Order any book as a high-quality paperback, elegant hardcover, or stunning boxset — and only pay what it costs to print. No markups. No middlemen.
- **Unlimited Access to the Greatest Works** - Enjoy thousands of timeless classics — from Plato to Shakespeare to Tolstoy — in beautiful, modern eBook and audiobook editions. Read and listen without limits — for every reader, everywhere.
- **Modern Translations for Every Language & Dialect** - We're reimagining the classics in clear, accessible language — and translating them into every dialect imaginable. Everyone deserves to understand humanity's greatest ideas.

When you visit **LibraryofAlexandria.com**, you're not just accessing books — you're joining a global movement to restore, preserve, and share the wisdom of civilization.

Join us today at LibraryofAlexandria.com

Together, we'll ensure the light of human wisdom never fades again.

With gratitude,

The Modern Library of Alexandria Team

Visit:
www.libraryofalexandria.com
Or scan the code below:

Introduction

Longfellow's Patriotic Vision and the Making of an American Legend

Henry Wadsworth Longfellow's *Paul Revere's Ride* is one of the most enduring and iconic poems in American literary history. First published in 1861, on the eve of the American Civil War, the poem immortalized the legendary midnight ride of April 18, 1775, when patriot Paul Revere set out to warn the colonial militias of the approaching British forces. While the historical facts of Revere's ride are well documented, Longfellow's poem is less a literal account than a stirring, Romanticized tribute to American bravery, resilience, and the spirit of revolution. In shaping this narrative, Longfellow transformed an already significant historical event into a national legend, embedding it in the collective memory of generations of Americans.

Longfellow's decision to write *Paul Revere's Ride* was deeply rooted in the political and social climate of the mid-19th century. At the time, the United States was deeply divided, with tensions between the North and South threatening to erupt into civil war. Longfellow, though not a politician or a soldier, used his pen to encourage a sense of unity and patriotism. By evoking the courage and sacrifice of the American Revolution, he sought to remind his readers of the shared values and struggles that had once united the colonies against a common enemy. In this sense, the poem functions not only as a retelling of history but also as a call to action, urging Americans to find strength in their collective past during a time of crisis.

The opening lines of the poem—"Listen, my children, and you shall hear / Of the midnight ride of Paul Revere"— immediately set the tone for a narrative that is both instructive and inspirational. The poem is structured as a dramatic ballad, with a rhythmic cadence that mirrors the galloping of Revere's horse and the urgency of his mission. Through vivid imagery and carefully chosen details, Longfellow captures the tension of that fateful night: the quiet of the sleeping villages, the stealth of the approaching British forces, and the lone rider who carries the fate of a nation on his shoulders. While the poem takes certain liberties with historical accuracy, its emotional truth—its celebration of courage, determination, and the fight for freedom—remains powerful and resonant.

Paul Revere himself is portrayed not just as a historical figure but as a symbol of American heroism. In Longfellow's narrative, he becomes a solitary sentinel, vigilant and unwavering in his duty to warn his fellow patriots. This portrayal aligns with the Romantic ideal of the individual hero, a figure who rises above fear and adversity to shape the course of history. By focusing on Revere's perspective and actions, Longfellow elevates a single moment into a timeless emblem of patriotic resolve.

Themes of Courage, Unity, and Revolutionary Spirit

At its core, *Paul Revere's Ride* is a poem about courage—the courage to act in the face of danger, to stand against oppression, and to fight for the ideals of liberty and independence. Longfellow's narrative emphasizes not only Revere's bravery but also the collective courage of the colonial militias, who were prepared to risk everything for the cause of freedom. The poem suggests that history is shaped not only by grand battles and political leaders but also by the actions of ordinary individuals who rise to extraordinary challenges.

Unity is another key theme. The poem highlights the interconnectedness of the colonial communities, with Revere's warning serving as the vital link that brings them together in a moment of crisis. The image of the signal lanterns—"One if by land, and two if by sea"—is both practical and symbolic, representing the network of communication and trust that underpinned the revolutionary movement. Longfellow's emphasis on this unity was particularly poignant in 1861, when the country was fracturing along regional lines. By recalling the shared sacrifices of the Revolutionary era, he sought to inspire a renewed sense of national solidarity.

The revolutionary spirit, with its blend of urgency, determination, and moral conviction, permeates the poem. Longfellow portrays the events of April 1775 not merely as a military skirmish but as a defining moment in the struggle for human freedom. The poem's language is charged with a sense of destiny, suggesting that the ride of Paul Revere was not just a historical event but a turning point in the larger narrative of liberty and justice. This sense of purpose is conveyed through the poem's relentless pace, its vivid contrasts between light and darkness, and its depiction of Revere as a lone voice crying out against tyranny.

Longfellow's handling of time and perspective also contributes to the poem's thematic richness. The narrative shifts fluidly between past and present, inviting readers to see the events of 1775 not as distant history but as a living legacy that continues to shape the nation's identity. By addressing his audience directly—"Listen, my children"—

Longfellow casts himself in the role of a bard or storyteller, preserving the memory of Revere's ride for future generations. This framing reinforces the idea that the values embodied by Revere's actions are timeless, belonging not only to the Revolutionary era but to every moment when freedom and justice are at stake.

Longfellow's Style and the Power of Storytelling

Longfellow's poetic style is characterized by its clarity, musicality, and emotional resonance, all of which are on full display in *Paul Revere's Ride*. The poem's meter and rhyme scheme create a rhythmic momentum that mirrors the urgency of Revere's mission. The repetition of sounds and phrases—such as the famous refrain about the signal lanterns—serves to anchor the narrative in the reader's memory, making it both memorable and impactful. This combination of narrative drive and lyrical beauty is one of the reasons why the poem has endured as a staple of American literature.

Imagery plays a crucial role in the poem's effectiveness. Longfellow's descriptions of the night—the moonlight glinting on the river, the darkened streets of the towns, the distant sounds of soldiers approaching—create a vivid and immersive atmosphere. These images are not merely decorative; they serve to heighten the tension and drama of the story, drawing the reader into the moment and making the stakes feel immediate and real. The contrast between light and darkness, in particular, functions as a symbolic motif, representing the struggle between freedom and tyranny, hope and fear.

Another notable aspect of Longfellow's style is his ability to blend historical narrative with Romantic idealism. While the poem is based on real events, Longfellow does not aim for strict historical accuracy. Instead, he crafts a narrative that captures the essence of the moment—the courage, the urgency, the sense of destiny—rather than its precise details. This approach allows him to create a work that is both historically rooted and universally resonant. Readers do not need to know every fact about Revere's ride to appreciate the poem's message; its emotional and symbolic power speaks for itself.

The enduring popularity of *Paul Revere's Ride* can be attributed in part to its role as a work of national mythology. Like many of Longfellow's poems, it seeks to define and celebrate the values that underpin American identity: bravery, independence, and a willingness to stand up for what is right. By transforming a historical episode into a narrative of heroism and moral clarity, Longfellow helped to shape the way Americans remember their revolutionary past. His poem has been recited in classrooms, quoted in speeches, and referenced in countless works of literature and popular culture, ensuring its place in the collective imagination of the nation.

For modern readers, *Paul Revere's Ride* offers both a glimpse into the historical struggles of the Revolutionary era and a timeless meditation on the nature of courage and freedom. It reminds us that history is not just a series of dates and events but a tapestry of human actions and choices, each of which has the power to shape the course of the future. As you read Longfellow's poem, consider not only the story it tells but also the values it celebrates—values that remain as relevant today as they were in 1775.

Paul Revere's Ride

Listen, my children, and you shall hear
Of the midnight ride of Paul Revere,
On the eighteenth of April, in Seventy-five;
Hardly a man is now alive
Who remembers that famous day and year.

He said to his friend, "If the British march
By land or sea from the town tonight,
Hang a lantern high in the belfry arch
Of the North Church tower as a signal light—
One, if by land, and two, if by sea;
And I on the opposite shore will be,
Ready to ride and spread the alarm
Through every Middlesex village and farm
For the country folk to be up and to arm."

Then he said, "Good night!" and with muffled oar
Silently rowed to the Charlestown shore,
Just as the moon rose over the bay,
Where swinging wide at her moorings lay
The Somerset, British man-of-war;
A phantom ship, with each mast and spar
Across the moon like a prison bar,
And a huge black hulk, that was magnified
By its own reflection in the tide.

Meanwhile, his friend, through alley and street,
Wanders and watches with eager ears,
Till in the silence around him he hears

The gathering of men at the barrack door,
The sound of arms, and the tramp of feet,
And the measured tread of the grenadiers,
Marching down to their boats on the shore.

Then he climbed the tower of the Old North Church,
By the wooden stairs, with stealthy tread,
To the belfry chamber overhead,
And startled the pigeons from their perch
On the dark rafters, that round him made
Masses and moving shapes of shade—
By the trembling ladder, steep and tall
To the highest window in the wall,
Where he paused to listen and look down
A moment on the roofs of the town,
And the moonlight flowing over all.

Beneath, in the churchyard, lay the dead,
In their night encampment on the hill,
Wrapped in silence so deep and still
That he could hear, like a sentinel's tread,
The watchful night wind, as it went
Creeping along from tent to tent
And seeming to whisper, "All is well!"
A moment only he feels the spell
Of the place and the hour, and the secret dread
Of the lonely belfry and the dead;
For suddenly all his thoughts are bent
On a shadowy something far away,
Where the river widens to meet the bay—
A line of black that bends and floats
On the rising tide, like a bridge of boats.

Meanwhile, impatient to mount and ride,
Booted and spurred, with a heavy stride
On the opposite shore walked Paul Revere.
Now he patted his horse's side,
Now gazed at the landscape far and near,
Then, restless, stamped the earth,
And turned and tightened his saddle girth;
But mostly he watched with eager search
The belfry tower of the Old North Church,
As it rose above the graves on the hill,
Lonely and ghostly and dark and still.
And look! as he watches, on the belfry's height
A glimmer, and then a gleam of light!
He springs to the saddle, the bridle he turns,
But lingers and gazes, till full on his sight
A second lamp in the belfry burns!

A hurry of hoofs in a village street,
A shape in the moonlight, a bulk in the dark,
And beneath, from the pebbles, in passing, a spark
Struck out by a steed flying fearless and fleet:
That was all! And yet, through the gloom and the light,
The fate of a nation was riding that night;
And the spark struck out by that steed, in his flight,
Kindled the land into flame with its heat.
He has left the village and mounted the steep,
And beneath him, tranquil and broad and deep,
Is the Mystic, meeting the ocean tides;
And under the alders, that skirt its edge,
Now soft on the sand, now loud on the ledge,
Is heard the tramp of his steed as he rides.

It was twelve by the village clock
When he crossed the bridge into Medford town.
He heard the crowing of the rooster,
And the barking of the farmer's dog,
And felt the damp of the river fog,
That rises after the sun goes down.

It was one by the village clock,
When he galloped into Lexington.
He saw the gilded weathercock
Swim in the moonlight as he passed,
And the meeting house windows, blank and bare,
Gaze at him with a ghostly glare,
As if they already stood aghast
At the bloody work they would look upon.

It was two by the village clock,
When he came to the bridge in Concord town.
He heard the bleating of the flock,
And the twitter of birds among the trees,
And felt the breath of the morning breeze
Blowing over the meadows brown.
And one was safe and asleep in his bed
Who at the bridge would be first to fall,
Who that day would be lying dead,
Pierced by a British musket ball.

You know the rest. In the books you have read,
How the British Regulars fired and fled—
How the farmers gave them ball for ball,
From behind each fence and farmyard wall,
Chasing the redcoats down the lane,
Then crossing the fields to emerge again

Under the trees at the turn of the road,
And only pausing to fire and load.

So through the night rode Paul Revere;
And so through the night went his cry of alarm
To every Middlesex village and farm—
A cry of defiance and not of fear,
A voice in the darkness, a knock at the door,
And a word that shall echo forevermore!
For, borne on the night wind of the Past,
Through all our history, to the last,
In the hour of darkness and peril and need,
The people will waken and listen to hear
The hurrying hoofbeats of that steed,
And the midnight message of Paul Revere.

Break

The Landlord finished his story,
Then stood up and took down from its hook
The sword that hung there, clouded with dust
And sticking to its sheath with rust,
And said, "This sword was in the battle."
The Poet grabbed it, and cried out,
"It is the sword of a good knight,
Though simple was his armor;
What does it matter if it isn't called
Joyeuse, Colada, Durindale,
Excalibur, or Aroundight,
Or other names the books mention?
Your ancestor, who carried this sword
As Colonel of the Volunteers,

Riding upon his old gray mare,
Spotted here and there and everywhere,
To me appears a grander figure
Than old Sir William, or whoever,
Clanking about in foreign lands
With iron gloves on his hands,
And on his head an iron helmet!"

Everyone laughed; the Landlord's face turned red
Like his coat of arms on the wall;
He could not understand at all
The meaning of what the Poet said;
For those who had been dead the longest
Were always greatest in his view;
And he was speechless with shock
To see Sir William's feathered head
Brought down to the same level as the rest,
And made the target of a joke.
And noticing this, to calm
The Landlord's anger, the others' worries,
The Student said, with relaxed confidence,
"The ladies and the gentlemen,
The weapons, the romances, the courtly manners,
The deeds of noble adventure, I sing!
Thus Ariosto speaks, in words
That have the dignified pace and sound
Of armored knights and clashing swords.
Now listen to the tale I bring
Listen! though I do not possess
The flowing elegance of his song,
The words that stir, the voice that enchants.
The Landlord's tale was one of warfare,
Only a tale of love is mine,

Mixing the human and divine,
A tale of the Decameron, told
In Palmieri's ancient garden,
By Fiametta, crowned with laurel,
While her companions lay around,
And heard the mingled sound
Of breezes that rushed on their missions,
And wild birds chattering overhead,
And whisper of leaves, and fountain's cascade,
And her own voice sweeter than all,
Telling the tale, which, lacking these,
Perhaps may lose its power to delight."

The Student's Tale

The Falcon of Ser Federigo

One summer morning, when the sun blazed hot, exhausted from working in his garden, Ser Federigo sat on a rough bench beneath his cottage eaves among the leaves of an enormous vine that spread its arms wide and hung its delicious clusters overhead. Below him, the river Arno flowed through the beautiful valley like a winding road, and from its banks rose high into the air the spires and rooftops of Florence the Fair—to him, a marble tomb that stood above his ruined fortunes and his buried love. For there, in banquets and tournaments, his wealth had been squandered, his fortune spent, trying to win and losing, since his courtship failed, Monna Giovanna, who married his rival, yet still reigned supreme in his imagination, the ideal woman of a young man's dreams.

Then he retreated, in poverty and pain, to this small farm, the last piece of his estate, his only comfort and his only concern to tend his vines and plant fig and pear trees; his only companion and only guest his falcon, faithful to him, when the rest, whose eager hands had once found so easy to lift the bronze knocker of his palace door, now lacked the strength to raise the wooden latch that gave entrance beneath a thatched roof. Companion of his lonely days, provider of his holiday feasts, on this bird the melancholy man bestowed the love that overflowed from his nature.

And so the empty years passed by, vacant yet filled with prophetic sounds, and so, that summer morning, he sat and pondered with folded, patient hands, as was his habit, and dreamily before his half-closed eyes floated the vision of his lost joy. Beside him, motionless, the sleepy bird dreamed of the hunt, and in his sleep heard the sudden, scythe-like sweep of wings that dared the headlong plunge through swirling gulfs of air, then, starting wide awake on his perch, jingled his bells like church bells at mass, and, looking at his master, seemed to say, "Ser Federigo, shall we hunt today?"

Ser Federigo wasn't thinking of the hunt; the tender vision of her lovely face—I won't say he seemed to see, he actually saw in the leaf-shadows of the trellises, herself, yet not herself; a beautiful child with flowing hair and wide, wild eyes, coming fearlessly up the garden path, looking not at him but at the hawk. "Beautiful falcon!" the child said, "I wish I could hold you on my wrist or see you fly!" The voice was hers and sent strange echoes through all the haunted chambers of his heart, like an aeolian harp pouring its wild music through the windy doors of some old ruin.

"Who is your mother, my fair boy?" he said, his hand resting gently on that shining head. "Monna Giovanna. Will

14

you let me stay a little while and play with your falcon? We live there, just beyond your garden wall, in the great house behind the tall poplars."

So the boy spoke on; and Federigo heard each softly spoken word as if from far away, and drifted onward through the golden gleams and shadows of the misty sea of dreams, like sailors becalmed drifting through vapors, feeling the sea beneath them rise and fall, hearing far off the mournful breakers roar and voices calling faintly from the shore! Then, waking from his pleasant daydreams, he took the little boy on his knees and told him stories of his brave bird, until in their friendship he became a third.

Monna Giovanna, widowed in her prime, had come with friends to spend the summer in her grand villa halfway up the hill, overlooking Florence but secluded and quiet; with iron gates that opened through long lines of sacred oak trees and ancient pines, and terraced gardens, and broad stone steps, and woodland deities overgrown with moss, and fountains pulsing in the heat, and all the Arno Valley stretched beneath its feet. Here in seclusion, as a widow may, the lovely lady passed the hours, pacing in black robes through the statue-filled hall, herself the most stately statue among all, and seeing more and more, with secret joy, her husband risen and living in her boy, until the lost sense of life returned again, not as delight but as relief from pain. Meanwhile the boy, rejoicing in his strength, stormed down the terraces from end to end; chased the screaming peacock in hot pursuit and climbed the garden trellises for fruit. But his chief pastime was watching the flight of a gerfalcon soaring into sight beyond the trees that bordered the garden wall, then swooping downward at some distant call; and as he gazed he often wondered who might be the master of the falcon, until that happy morning when he found master and falcon in the cottage yard.

And now a shadow and terror fell on the great house, as if a funeral bell tolled from the tower and filled each spacious room with secret dread and supernatural gloom; the pampered boy grew ill, and day by day wasted away with mysterious sickness. The mother's heart would not be comforted; her darling seemed to her already dead, and often, sitting by the sufferer's side, "What can I do to comfort you?" she cried. At first the silent lips made no reply, but moved at length by her persistent cry, "Give me," he answered with pleading tone, "Ser Federigo's falcon for my own!" No answer could the astonished mother make; how could she ask, even for her darling's sake, such a favor from an unlucky lover's hand, well knowing that to ask was to command? Well knowing what all falconers admitted, in all the land that falcon was the best, the master's pride and passion and delight, and the sole companion of this poor knight. But yet, for her child's sake, she could do no less than agree to soothe his restlessness, so promised, and then promising to keep her promise sacred, watched him fall asleep.

The next day was a bright September morning; the earth was beautiful as if newborn; there was that nameless splendor everywhere, that wild excitement in the air, which makes passersby in the city street congratulate each other as they meet. Two lovely ladies, dressed in cloak and hood, passed through the garden gate into the wood, under the lustrous leaves and through the gleam of dewy sunshine streaming down between.

The one, closely hooded, had the attractive grace which sorrow sometimes gives a woman's face; her dark eyes moistened with the mists that roll from the gulf-stream of passion in the soul; the other with her hood thrown back, her hair making a golden glory in the air, her cheeks flushed with a rosy blush, her young heart singing louder than the thrush. So walked, that morning, through mingled light and shade, each made more beautiful by the other's presence, Monna Giovanna and her dearest friend, focused on their errand and its purpose.

They found Ser Federigo at his work, like banished Adam, digging in the soil; and when he looked and saw these fair women, the garden suddenly was glorified; his long-lost Eden was restored again, and the strange river winding through the plain no longer was the Arno to his eyes, but the Euphrates watering Paradise!

Monna Giovanna raised her stately head and with gracious words of greeting said: "Ser Federigo, we come here as friends, hoping in this to make some small amends for past unkindness. I who never before would even cross the threshold of your door, I who in happier days maintained such pride, refused your banquets and scorned your gifts, this morning come, a self-invited guest, to test your generous nature, and breakfast with you under your own vine." To which he answered: "Poor merit of mine, don't call it your unkindness, for if anything is good in me of feeling or of thought, it comes from you, and this last grace outweighs all sorrows, all regrets of other days."

And after further compliments and conversation, among the asters in the garden walk he left his guests; and to his cottage turned, and as he entered for a moment longed for the lost splendors of the days of old, the ruby glass, the silver and the gold, and felt how piercing is the sting of pride, made bitter and intensified by want. He looked around for some means or way to celebrate this unexpected holiday; searched every cupboard, and then searched again, called the maid, who came but came in vain; "The master didn't hunt today," she said, "there's nothing in the house but wine and bread."

Then suddenly the sleepy falcon shook his little bells, with that knowing look, which said, as plain as spoken words, "If anything is needed, I am here!" Yes, everything is needed, brave bird! The master seized you without another word. Like your own lure, he whirled you around; ah me! The pomp and flutter of brave falconry, the bells, the jesses, the bright scarlet hood, the flight and the pursuit over field and wood, all these forevermore are ended now; no longer victor, but the victim you!

Then on the table a snow-white cloth he spread, laid on its wooden dish the loaf of bread, brought purple grapes warm with autumn sunshine, the fragrant peach, the juicy bergamot; then in the center a flask of wine he placed, and with autumn flowers graced the banquet. Ser Federigo, would not these suffice without your falcon stuffed with cloves and spice?

When all was ready, and the courtly lady with her companion came to the cottage, upon Ser Federigo's mind there fell the wild enchantment of a magic spell! The room they entered, humble and low and small, was transformed into a sumptuous banquet hall, with fanfares blown by aerial trumpets; the rustic chair she sat on was a throne; he ate heavenly food, and a divine flavor was given to his country wine, and the poor falcon, fragrant with his spice, was a peacock, or bird of paradise!

When the meal was finished, they arose and passed again into the garden enclosure. Then said the lady, "Far too well I know, remembering still the days of long ago, though you don't betray it, with what surprise you see me here in this familiar way. You have no children, and you cannot guess what anguish, what unspeakable distress a mother feels whose child is lying ill, nor how her heart anticipates his will. And yet for this, you see me lay aside all womanly reserve and restraint of pride, and ask the thing most precious in your sight, your falcon, your sole comfort and delight, which if you find it in your heart to give, my poor, unhappy boy perhaps may live."

Ser Federigo listens and replies, with tears of love and pity in his eyes: "Alas, dear lady! there can be no task so sweet to me as giving when you ask. One little hour ago, if I had known this wish of yours, it would have been my own. But thinking in what manner I could best honor the presence of my guest, I deemed that nothing worthier could be than what was most dear and precious to me, and so my gallant falcon breathed his last to provide this morning our meal."

In silent regret, mixed with dismay, the gentle lady turned her eyes away, grieving that he should make such sacrifice and kill his falcon for a woman's sake, yet feeling in her heart a woman's pride that nothing she could ask for was denied; then took her leave and passed out at the gate with slow footstep and disconsolate soul.

Three days went by, and lo! a funeral bell tolled from the little chapel in the dell; ten strokes Ser Federigo heard, and said, breathing a prayer, "Alas! her child is dead!" Three months went by; and lo! a merrier chime rang from the chapel bells at Christmas time; the cottage was deserted, and no more Ser Federigo sat beside its door, but now, with servants to do his will, in the grand villa halfway up the hill, sat at the Christmas feast, and at his side Monna Giovanna, his beloved bride, never so beautiful, so kind, so fair, enthroned once more in the old rustic chair, high-perched upon the back of which there stood the image of a falcon

carved in wood, and underneath the inscription, with date,
"All things come round to him who will but wait."

As soon as the story came to its end,
One person, too eager to praise,
Heaped upon it unwise acclaim;
And then voices of criticism emerged,
Fanning the sparks of disagreement
Into a rather heated debate.

The Theologian shook his head;
"These old Italian stories," he said,
"From the highly celebrated Decameron onward
Through all the crowd of others,
Are either trivial, boring, or crude;
The chatter of a community
In some distant country town,
A shameful record at its finest!
They strike me as a stagnant marsh,
Overgrown with rushes and reeds,
Where a white lily, occasionally,
Flowers among the poisonous weeds
And deadly nightshade along its edges."

To this the Student immediately responded,
"For the white lily, much appreciation!
One should not declare, with excessive arrogance,
Fountain, I will not drink from you!
Nor would it be thankful to overlook,
That from these pools and reservoirs
Even the great Shakespeare drew
His Moor of Venice, and the Jew,

And Romeo and Juliet,
And many a celebrated comedy."
Then a long silence fell; until someone finally spoke,
"An Angel is flying overhead!"
Upon hearing these words, the Spanish Jew responded,
And whispered with a quiet breath:
"God grant, if what you say is true,
It may not be the Angel of Death!"
And then another silence; and then,
Stroking his beard, he spoke once more:
"This brings back to my mind
A story told in the Talmud,
That book of treasures, that book of gold,
Of wonders countless and varied,
A tale that frequently returns to me,
And fills my heart, and occupies my thoughts,
And never grows tiresome nor becomes old."

THE END

Thank You For Reading

You've Just Read a Piece of the Greatest Library Ever Rebuilt

Thank you for reading.

This book is one of thousands we're restoring, reimagining, and translating as part of the **Modern Library of Alexandria** — a global movement to preserve and share humanity's most important ideas.

What was once lost to fire and time is now rising again — not just as memory, but as living, breathing knowledge, freely accessible to all.

What You Can Do Next:

- **Keep Reading.**

  Discover more legendary works — in beautiful print, audiobook, or digital form — at LibraryofAlexandria.com.

- **Build Your Own Library.**

  Every title is available as a paperback, hardcover, or collectible boxset — at true printing cost. Craft a personal library worthy of display.

- **Spread the Light.**

  Share this book. Tell others about the movement. Help us translate every timeless work into every language, so no reader is ever left behind.

By finishing this book, you've already taken part in something extraordinary.

Join us at LibraryofAlexandria.com

Together, we're rebuilding the greatest library the world has ever known.

With appreciation,

The Modern Library of Alexandria Team

Visit:
www.libraryofalexandria.com
Or scan the code below: